9/06

Easy
JBIO
Roosevelt

# Table of Contents

Early Years . . . . . . . . . . . . . . . 5

Eleanor and Franklin . . . . . . . 11

First Lady . . . . . . . . . . . . . 15

Later Years . . . . . . . . . . . 19


Glossary . . . . . . . . . . . . 22

Read More . . . . . . . . . . . 23

Internet Sites . . . . . . . . . . 23

Index/Word List . . . . . . . . . 24

## Time Line

1884
born

# Early Years

Eleanor Roosevelt worked for peace and human rights. She was born in 1884 in New York. Her parents died when she was young. Eleanor lived with her grandmother.

◀ Eleanor at age 5

## Time Line

1884
born

1899
attends school
in England

In 1899, Eleanor went to school in England. She was very smart. Eleanor learned that it was important to care about others. She visited many countries in Europe.

Eleanor with classmates at Allenswood Academy in England in 1900

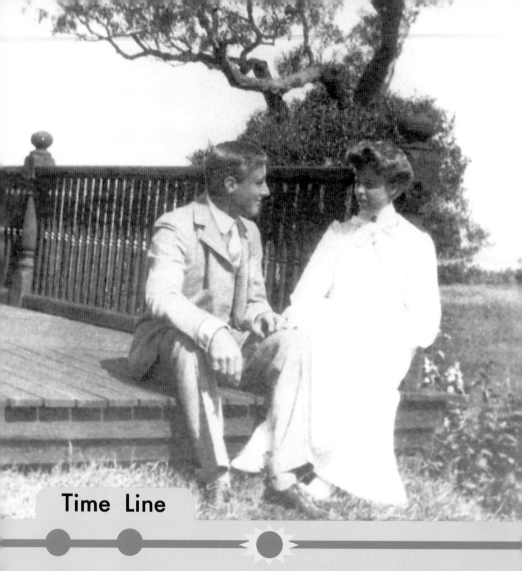

## Time Line

1884
born

1899
attends school
in England

1905
marries Franklin
Roosevelt

Eleanor came back to New York in 1902. She taught children. She worked to make women's jobs better. In 1905, Eleanor married Franklin Roosevelt. Franklin was her distant cousin.

## Time Line

1884
born

1899
attends school
in England

1905
marries Franklin
Roosevelt

# Eleanor and Franklin

Eleanor and Franklin had six children. One child died. The family moved to Washington, D.C., in 1913. Franklin worked for the U.S. Navy. Eleanor volunteered with the Red Cross.

## Time Line

| | | | |
|---|---|---|---|
| 1884 born | 1899 attends school in England | 1905 marries Franklin Roosevelt | 1926 starts furniture company |

Eleanor and three friends started a company in 1926. The company gave jobs to young people. The workers learned how to weave and make furniture.

Eleanor (left) helping a worker at her company called Val-Kill Industries

## Time Line

1884
born

1899
attends school
in England

1905
marries Franklin
Roosevelt

1926
starts furniture
company

# First Lady

Eleanor became first lady when Franklin became president of the United States in 1933.

1933
becomes
first lady

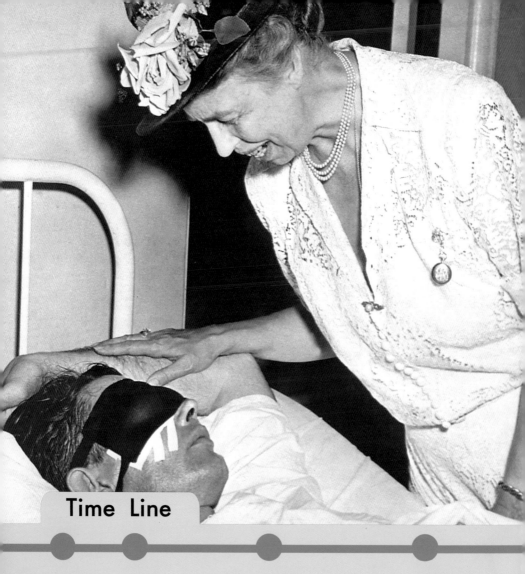

## Time Line

1884
born

1899
attends school
in England

1905
marries Franklin
Roosevelt

1926
starts furnitu
company

As first lady, Eleanor traveled to many places. She visited hospitals, prisons, and schools. Eleanor and Franklin talked about what she learned.

◄ Eleanor visiting a soldier at a hospital in 1944

1933
becomes
first lady

## Time Line

1884
born

1899
attends school
in England

1905
marries Franklin
Roosevelt

1926
starts furniture
company

# Later Years

In 1945, Eleanor worked at the United Nations. She helped write a paper on human rights. Eleanor believed that all people should be treated equally.

1933
becomes
first lady

1945
works at
United Nations

## Time Line

1884
born

1899
attends school
in England

1905
marries Franklin
Roosevelt

1926
starts furnitu
company

Eleanor wrote many books
and articles. She died
in 1962. People remember
Eleanor for her kindness
and her work for peace.

| 1933 | 1945 | 1962 |
|------|------|------|
| becomes first lady | works at United Nations | dies |

# Glossary

**article**—a piece of writing printed in a newspaper or magazine

**human rights**—the idea that all people should be treated fairly

**Red Cross**—an organization that gives food, clothing, and money to people after floods, earthquakes, war, and other terrible events

**United Nations**—a group of countries around the world that works for peace; Eleanor helped write the Universal Declaration of Human Rights when she was a delegate to the United Nations.

**volunteer**—to offer to do a job without pay

# Read More

**Koestler-Grack, Rachel A.** *The Story of Eleanor Roosevelt.* Breakthrough Biographies. Philadelphia: Chelsea Clubhouse, 2004.

**Rosenberg, Pam.** *Eleanor Roosevelt.* Early Biographies. Minneapolis: Compass Point Books, 2003.

**Stone, Amy.** *Eleanor Roosevelt.* Raintree Biographies. Austin, Texas: Raintree Steck-Vaughn, 2003.

# Internet Sites

FactHound offers a safe, fun way to find Internet sites related to this book. All of the sites on FactHound have been researched by our staff.

Here's how:

1. Visit *www.facthound.com*
2. Type in this special code **0736820809** for age-appropriate sites. Or enter a search word related to this book for a more general search.
3. Click on the **Fetch It** button.

FactHound will fetch the best sites for you!

# Index/Word List

articles, 21
books, 21
born, 5
children, 9, 11
company, 13
cousin, 9
England, 7
Europe, 7
first lady, 15, 17

furniture, 13
human rights, 5, 19
married, 9
New York, 5, 9
paper, 19
parents, 5
peace, 5, 21
Red Cross, 11

Roosevelt, Franklin, 9, 11, 15, 17
school, 7, 17
taught, 9
United Nations, 19
visited, 7, 17
Washington, D.C., 11

**Word Count: 221**
**Early-Intervention Level: 18**

**Editorial Credits**

Sarah L. Schuette, editor; Heather Kindseth, cover designer and illustrator; Enoch Peterson, production designer; Kelly Garvin, photo researcher; Karen Hieb, product planning editor

**Photo Credits**

Corbis, 4, 12; Underwood & Underwood, 14; Bettmann, 16, 18, 20
Franklin D. Roosevelt Library, cover, 1, 6 (both), 8, 10